JUST FOR FUN

EASY ROCK MANDOLIN

12 GREAT ROCK SONGS—JUST A FEW CHORDS

ARRANGED BY AARON STANG AND ANDREW DUBROCK

 Alfred

Produced by
Alfred Music Publishing Co., Inc.
P.O. Box 10003
Van Nuys, CA 91410-0003
alfred.com

Printed in USA.

ISBN-10: 0-7390-6462-2
ISBN-13: 978-0-7390-6462-7

Cover Photos
Central image models: Katrina Hruschka and Andrew Callahan / Photographer: Brian Immke, www.adeptstudios.com
Mandolin: courtesy of Gibson USA • Moon: courtesy of The Library of Congress • Gramophone: © istockphoto / Faruk Tasdemir
MP3 player: © istockphoto / tpopova • Microphone: © istockphoto / Graffizone • Handstand: © istockphoto / jhorrocks
Jumping woman: © istockphoto / Dan Wilton • Woman and radio: courtesy of The Library of Congress • Sneakers: © istockphoto / ozgurdonmaz
Background: image copyright Elise Gravel, 2009, used under license from Shutterstock.com

 Contents printed on 100% recycled paper.

FOREWORD

Easy Rock Mandolin is designed for your total enjoyment. Each featured song is inherently simple, with just a few chords. All the tunes are arranged for mandolin from the actual guitar parts, simplified just enough to keep them fun and musically satisfying. Make sure to listen to the original recordings so you know how these parts should sound before you start trying to learn them. But most important, just have fun!

—Aaron Stang, Arranger and Editor
Alfred Music Publishing Co., Inc.

CONTENTS

AS TEARS GO BY

Words and Music by
MICK JAGGER, KEITH RICHARDS
and ANDREW LOOG OLDHAM

As Tears Go By - 2 - 1

CASEY JONES

Words by
ROBERT HUNTER

Music by
JERRY GARCIA

Medium tempo ♩ = 92

Rhy. Fig. 1

end Rhy. Fig. 1

Cont. in slashes

Chorus:

Driv - ing that train,___ high on co - caine,___

Ca - sey Jones,_ you'd bet - ter watch your speed.___

Cont. rhy. simile

Trou - ble a - head,___ trou - ble be - hind,___ and you know that no - tion

w/Rhy. Fig. 1

just crossed my mind.___

Verse:

1. This old en - gine makes it on time,___ leaves Cen - tral Sta - tion 'bout a
2. Trou - ble a - head, the la - dy in red,___ take my ad - vice___ you'd be
3. *Instrumental*
4. *See additional lyrics*

Casey Jones - 2 - 1

Verse 4:
Trouble with you is the trouble with me,
Got two good eyes but you still don't see.
Come 'round the bend, you know it's the end,
The fireman screams and the engine just gleams.
(To Chorus:)

GIMME SOME LOVIN'

Words and Music by
STEVE WINWOOD, MUFF WINWOOD
and SPENCER DAVIS

Moderately fast ♩ = 147

Intro:

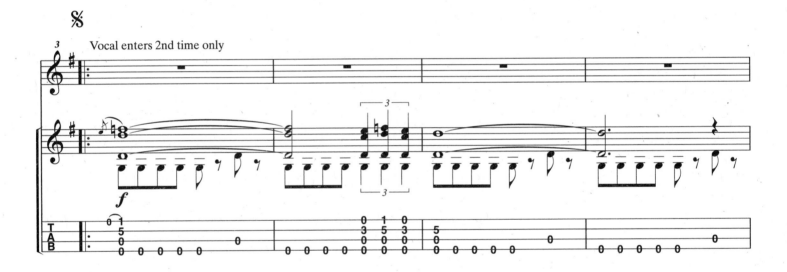

Vocal enters 2nd time only

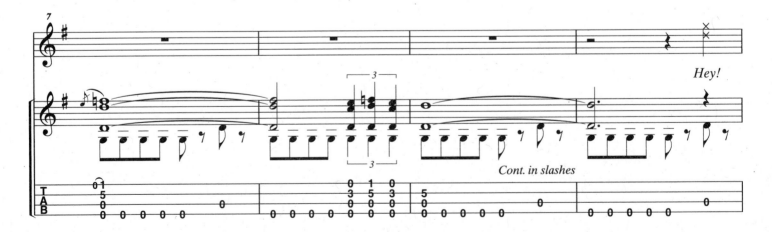

Gimme Some Lovin' - 4 - 1

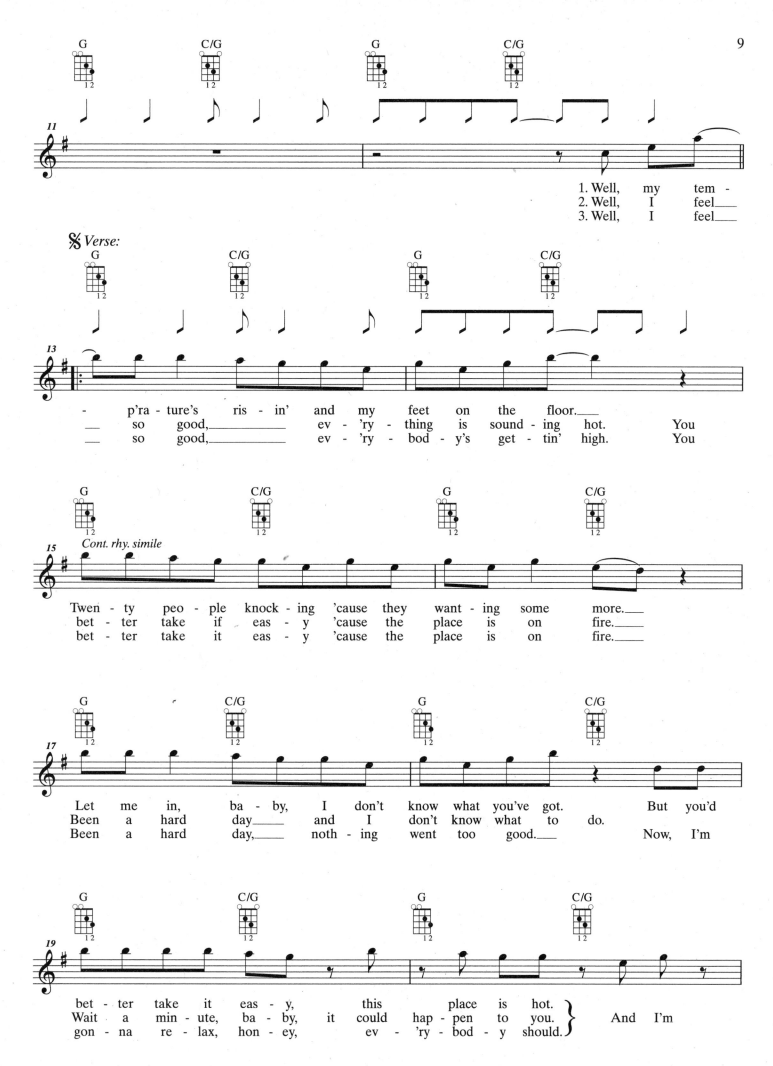

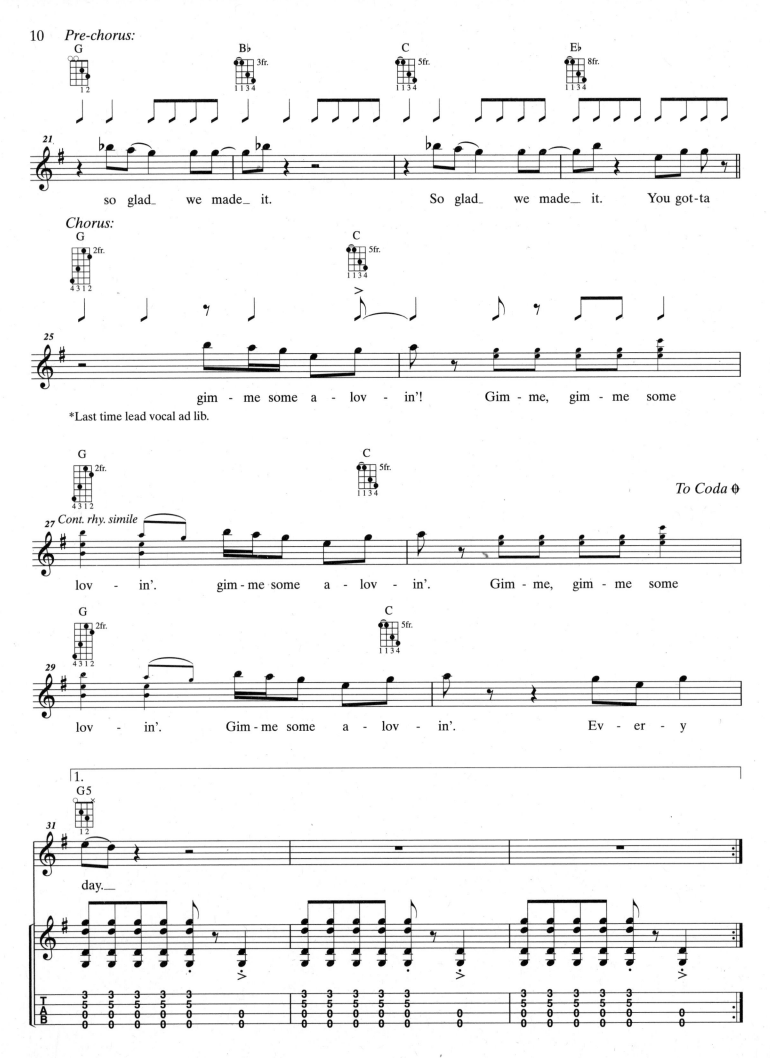

Pre-chorus:

so glad_ we made_ it. So glad_ we made_ it. You got-ta

Chorus:

gim - me some a - lov - in'! Gim - me, gim - me some

*Last time lead vocal ad lib.

Cont. rhy. simile

lov - in'. gim - me some a - lov - in'. Gim - me, gim - me some

lov - in'. Gim - me some a - lov - in'. Ev - er - y

To Coda

day.___

GLORIA

Words and Music by
VAN MORRISON

Moderately ♩ = 124

Intro:

1. I'd like to tell you 'bout my

Verse:

Cont. rhy. simile

ba - by,

you know, she comes a - round.

2. *See additional lyrics*

Just a-bout five feet four,

from her head to the ground.

You know, she comes a-round here,

just a - bout mid - night.

She make you feel so good,

Gloria - 4 - 1

she make you feel al - right.

1.

And her name is G - l - o -

- r - i - i - i - a,

To Next Strain 2.
(To Chorus:)

G - l - o - r - i - a.   G - l - o - r - i - a.

Chorus:

Cont. rhy. simile

G - l - o - r - i - a.

(Glo - ri - a.   Glo - ri - a.)

I'm gon - na shout_ it all night.   I'm gon - na shout_ it ev-'ry day.

(Glo - ri - a.

To Coda

Yeah, yeah,_ yeah, yeah, yeah, yeah.

Glo - ri - a.)

Instrumental:

2. She comes a-round   here,

⊕ *Coda*

yeah, yeah, yeah. So good.___ Al-right, feels so good.__

(Glo - ri - a.___)

(Glo - ri - a.) Oh, al-right.__ Hey,_ now.

Verse 2: (Half Spoken)
She comes around here
Just about midnight.
She make me feel so good,
I wanna say she make me feel alright.
Comes walkin' down my street,
Watch her come to my house.
She knocks upon my door,
And then she comes to my room.
Then she makes me feel alright,
G-l-o-r-i-a.
(To Chorus:)

BIG YELLOW TAXI

Words and Music by
JONI MITCHELL

Big Yellow Taxi - 3 - 1

Verse:

paved par - a - dise,___ put up a park - ing lot.___

2.3.4. *See additional lyrics*

*Use alternating E–E6 pattern as in intro figure.

With a pink___ ho - tel,___ a bou - tique, and a swing-ing___

Chorus:

___ hot___ spot.___ Don't it al - ways seem_

___ to go that you don't know what_ you've got___ till it's gone. They

paved par - a - dise, put up a park - ing lot.___

1.2.3.

2. They

Verse 2:
They took all the trees,
Put 'em in a tree museum.
And they charged the people
A dollar and a half just to see 'em.
(To Chorus:)

Verse 3:
Hey farmer, farmer,
Put away that DDT now.
Give me spots on my apples,
But leave me the birds and the bees,
Please!
(To Chorus:)

Verse 4:
Late last night
I heard the screen door slam.
And a big yellow taxi
Took away my old man.
(To Chorus:)

GOOD RIDDANCE (TIME OF YOUR LIFE)

Lyrics by
BILLIE JOE

Music by
BILLIE JOE and GREEN DAY

1. An-oth-er turn-ing point, a fork stuck in the road.
2. So take the pho-to-graphs and still frames in your mind.
3. *Instrumental*

Time grabs you by the wrist, di-rects you where to go.
Hang it on a shelf in good health and good time.

So make the best of this test and don't ask why.
Tat-toos of mem-o-ries, and dead skin on trial.

It's not a ques-tion, but a les-son learned in time. It's
For what it's worth, it was worth all the while.

Good Riddance (Time of Your Life) - 3 - 1

20

Chorus:

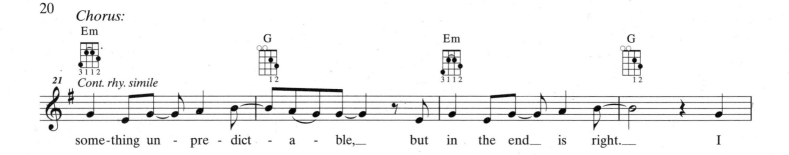

some-thing un - pre - dict - a - ble,__ but in the end__ is right.__ I

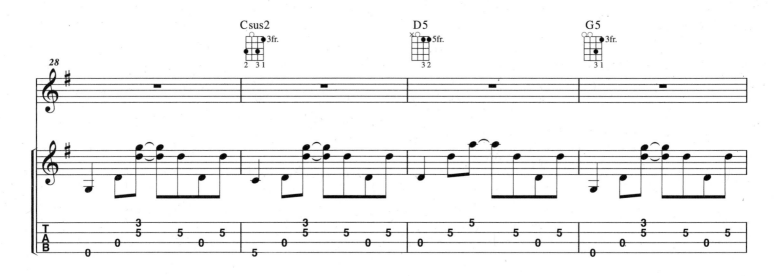

hope you had__ the time_____ of__ your life.__

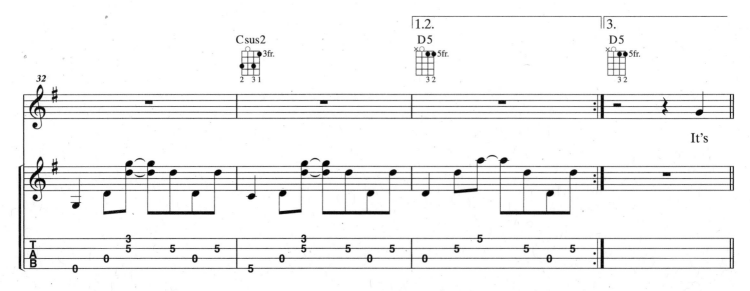

It's

Good Riddance (Time of Your Life) - 3 - 2

some - thing un - pre - dict - a - ble,___ but in the end___ is right.___

___ I hope you had___ the time_____ of___ your life.___

A HORSE WITH NO NAME

Words and Music by
DEWEY BUNNELL

A Horse with No Name - 3 - 1

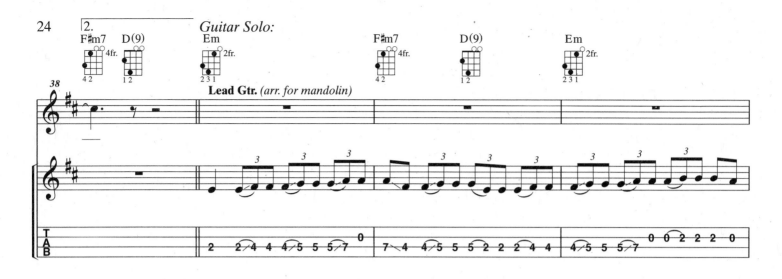

Guitar Solo:

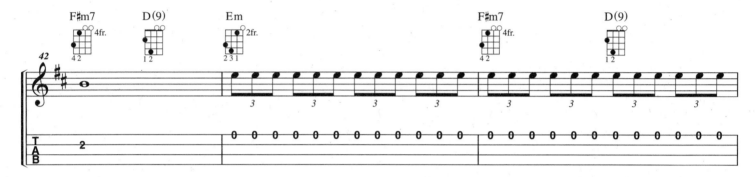

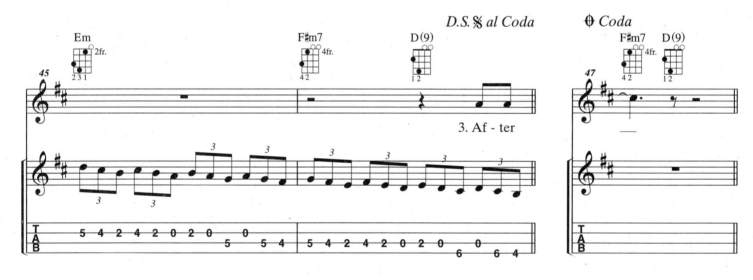

La la la la la la la la la la la. La

Verse 2:
After two days in the desert sun
My skin began to turn red.
After three days in the desert fun
I was looking at a river bed.
And the story it told of a river that flowed
Made me sad to think it was dead.
You see, I've…
(To Chorus:)

Verse 3:
After nine days I let the horse run free
'Cause the desert had turned to sea.
There were plants and birds and rocks and things,
There were sand and hills and rings.
The ocean is a desert with its life underground
And the perfect disguise above.
Under the cities lies a heart made of ground,
But the humans will give no love.
You see, I've…
(To Chorus:)

MARGARITAVILLE

Words and Music by
JIMMY BUFFETT

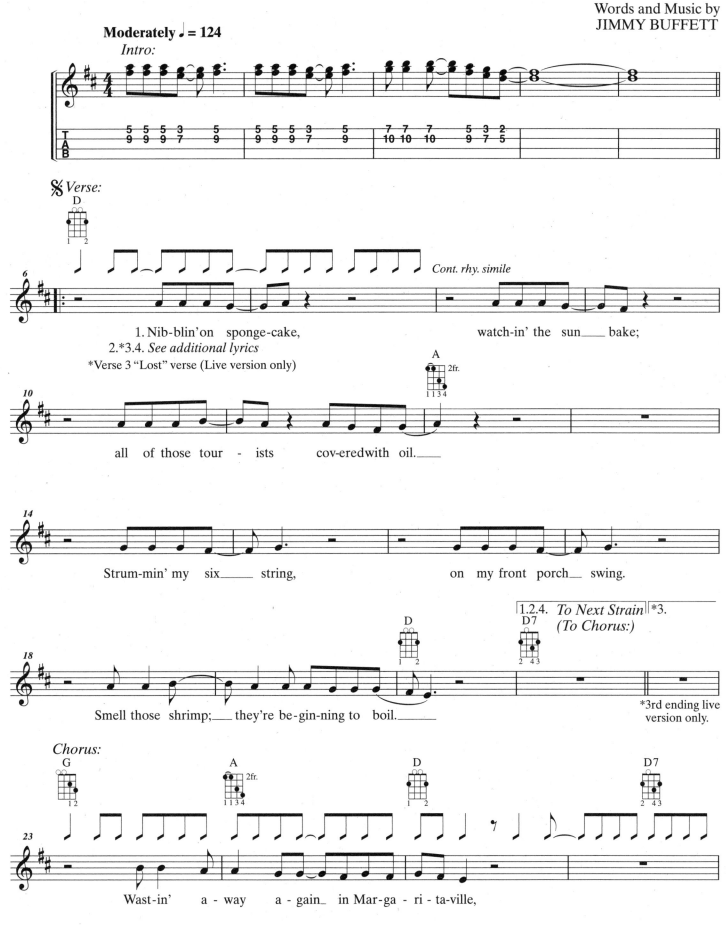

Margaritaville - 3 - 1

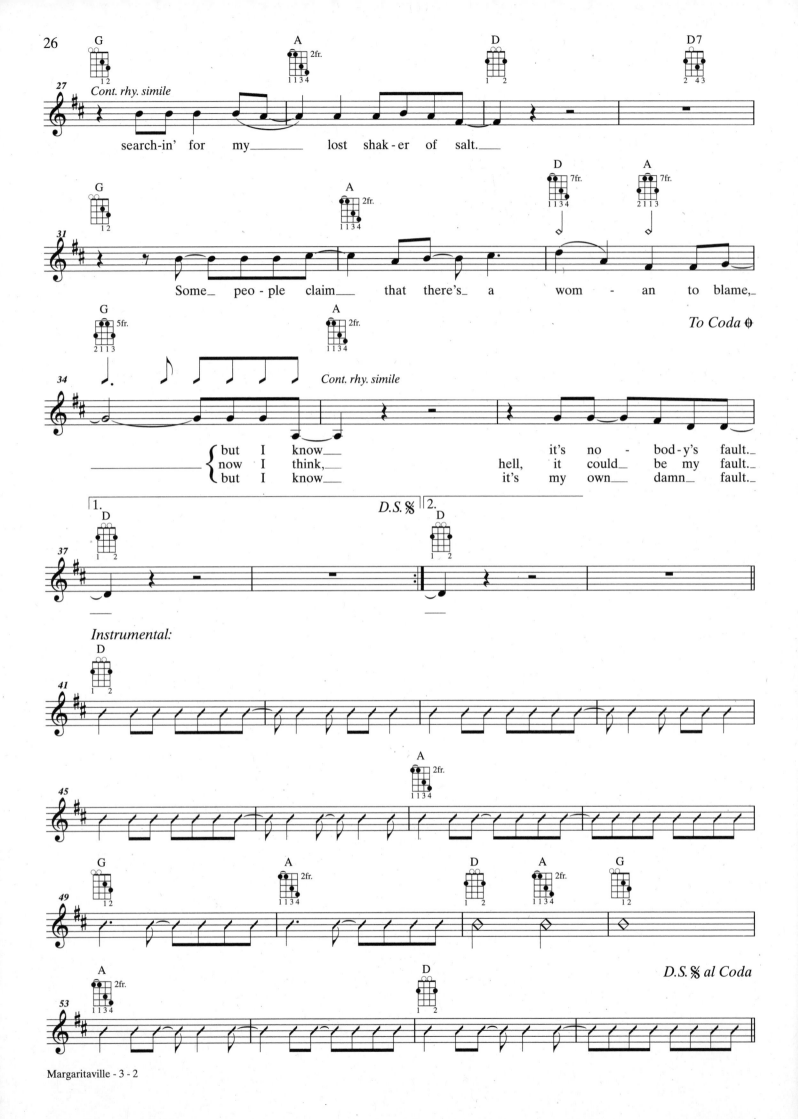

⊕ *Coda*

Yes, and some peo-ple claim__ that there's__ a wom-an to blame_____ and I know__ it's my own__ damn__ fault.__

Verse 2:
Don't know the reason,
I stayed here all season
With nothing to show but this brand-new tattoo.
But it's a real beauty,
A Mexican cutie,
How it got here I haven't a clue.
(To Chorus:)

Verse 3:
Old men in tank tops
Cruising the gift shops
Checking out the chiquitas down by the shore.
They dream about weight loss,
Wish they could be their own boss.
Those three-day vacations become such a bore.

*"Lost" verse (Live version only)

Verse 4:
I blew out my flip-flop,
Stepped on a pop-top;
Cut my heel, had to cruise on back home.
But there's booze in the blender,
And soon it will render
That frozen concoction that helps me hang on.
(To Chorus:)

PEACEFUL EASY FEELING

Words and Music by
JACK TEMPCHIN

Verse 2:
And I found out a long time ago
What a woman can do to your soul.
Ah, but she can't take you anyway,
You don't already know how to go.
(To Chorus:)

Verse 3:
Instrumental

Verse 4:
I get this feelin' I may know you
As a lover and a friend.
But this voice keeps whispering in my other ear,
Tells me I may never see you again.
(To Chorus:)

TAKE IT EASY

Words and Music by
JACKSON BROWNE
and GLENN FREY

Moderately ♩ = 138
Intro:

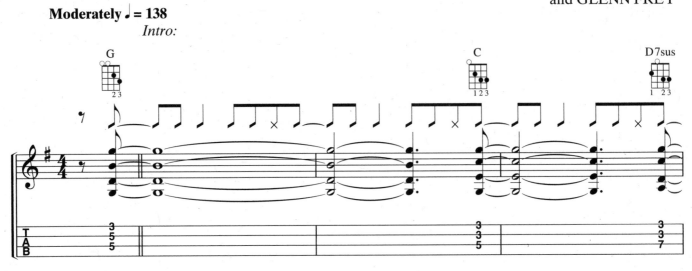

1.Well, I'm a-

Take It Easy - 4 - 1

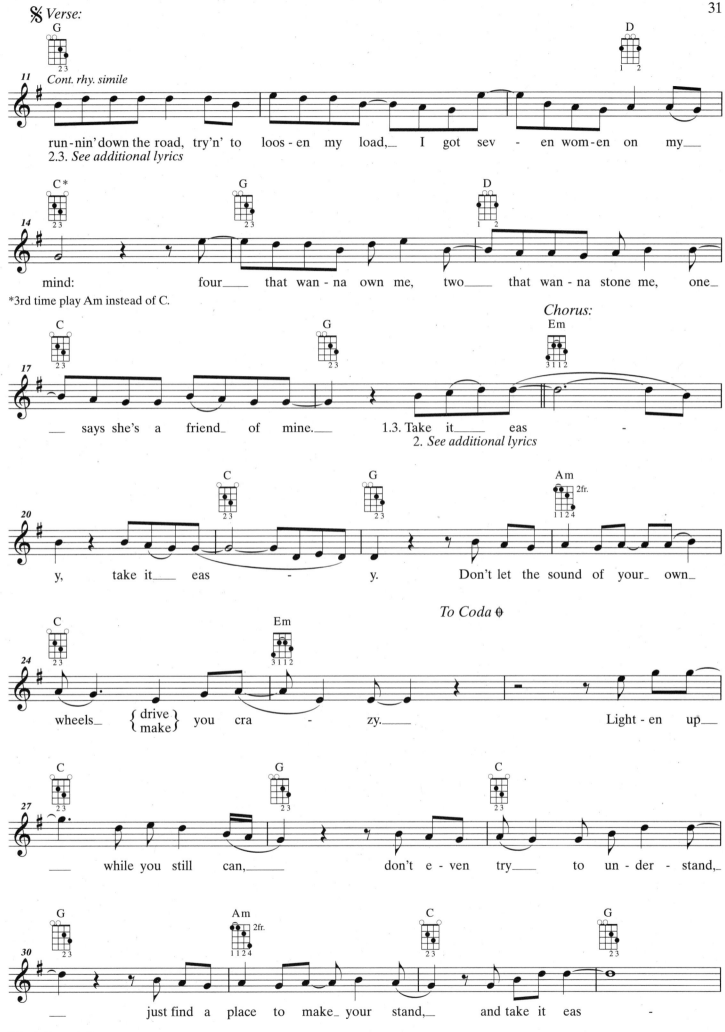

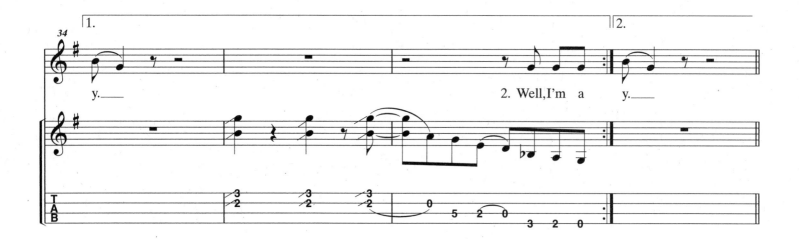

Guitar Solo:

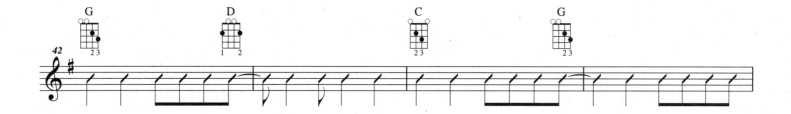

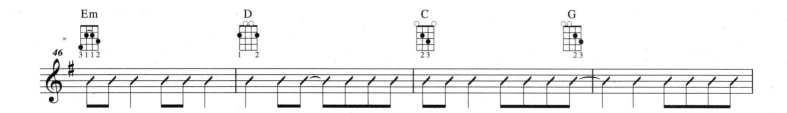

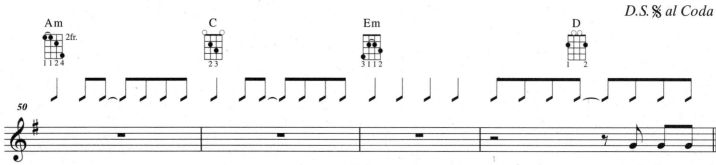

D.S. % al Coda

3. Well, I'm a -

⊕ Coda

Outro:

Resume Verse rhy. simile

Ooh,_____ ooh,_____ ooh,_____ ooh. Ooh,_____

ooh,_____ ooh,_____ ooh._____ Ooh,_____ Oh,_ we got it
(Ooh._____)

eas - y. We ought-ta take it

eas - y.

Verse 2:
Well, I'm a-standin' on a corner in Winslow, Arizona,
And such a fine sight to see:
It's a girl, my Lord, in a flatbed Ford
Slowin' down to take a look at me.

Chorus 2:
Come on, baby, don't say maybe.
I gotta know if your sweet love is gonna save me.
We may lose and we may win, though we will never be here again.
So open up, I'm climbin' in, so take it easy.
(To Guitar Solo:)

Verse 3:
Well, I'm a-runnin' down the road, tryin' to loosen my load,
Got a world of trouble on my mind.
Lookin' for a lover who won't blow my cover,
She's so hard to find.
(To Chorus:)

MOONDANCE

Words and Music by
VAN MORRISON

TAKE ME HOME, COUNTRY ROADS

Words and Music by
JOHN DENVER, BILL DANOFF
and TAFFY NIVERT

Moderately bright in 2 ♩ = 86

Intro:

mf
hold throughout

Verse:

Cont. simile

1. Al - most heav - en,___ West Vir - gin - ia,
2. All my mem - 'ries___ gath - er 'round__ her,

Blue Ridge Moun - tains, Shen - an - do - ah Riv - er.___
min - er's la - dy,___ strang - er to blue wa - ter.___

Life is old___ there, old - er than__ the___ trees,
Dark and dust - y, paint - ed on___ the___ sky,

young - er than__ the moun - tains blow - in' like a breeze.
mist - y taste__ of__ moon - shine, tear - drop in my eye.___ } Coun - try roads,___

Take Me Home, Country Roads - 3 - 1

Chorus:

A CHORDS

A
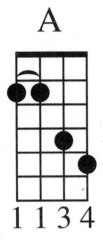
1 1 3 4

A
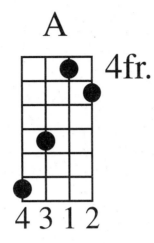
4fr.
4 3 1 2

Amaj7

1 1 3 3

A6
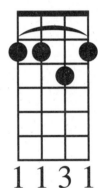
1 1 3 1

Am

1 1 2 4

Am
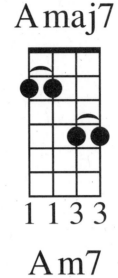
3fr.
2 4 1 3

Am7
1 1 3 3

Am6
1 1 3 1

A7
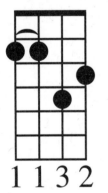
1 1 3 2

A7
4fr.
4 2 1 3

A9
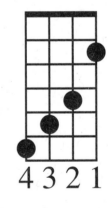
4fr.
3 2 1 4

A13
4 3 2 1

Asus
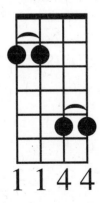
1 1 4 4

A7sus
1 1 4 2

Adim7

2 1 4 3

A+

1 2 3 4

B♭ (A♯) CHORDS*

B♭

1 1 3 4

B♭
 5fr.
4 3 1 2

B♭maj7
1 1 3 3

B♭6
1 1 3 1

B♭m

1 1 2 4

B♭m
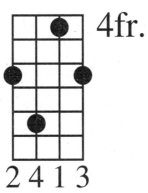 4fr.
2 4 1 3

B♭m7
1 1 3 3

B♭m6

1 1 3 1

B♭7
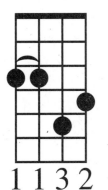
1 1 3 2

B♭7
 5fr.
4 2 1 3

B♭9
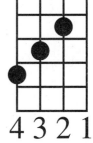 5fr.
3 2 1 4

B♭13
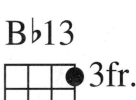 3fr.
4 3 2 1

B♭sus
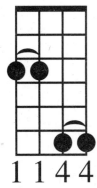
1 1 4 4

B♭7sus
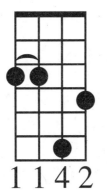
1 1 4 2

B♭dim7
2 1 4 3

B♭+

1 2 3 4

*B♭ and A♯ are two names for the same note.

B CHORDS

B
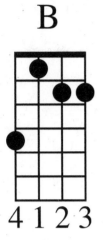
4 1 2 3

B
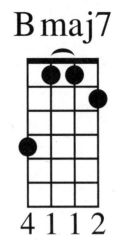
4fr.
1 1 3 4

Bmaj7
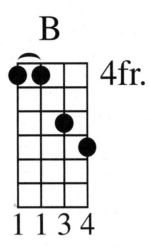
4 1 1 2

B6
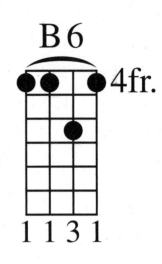
4fr.
1 1 3 1

Bm
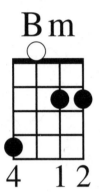
4   1 2

Bm
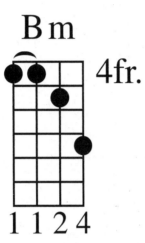
4fr.
1 1 2 4

Bm7
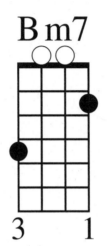
3   1

Bm6
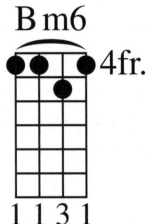
4fr.
1 1 3 1

B7
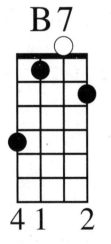
4 1   2

B7
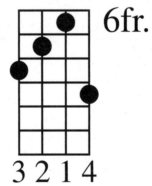
4fr.
1 1 3 2

B9
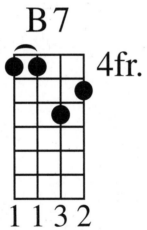
6fr.
3 2 1 4

B13
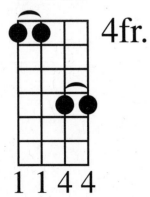
4fr.
4 3 2 1

Bsus
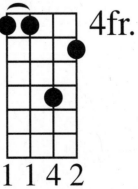
4fr.
1 1 4 4

B7sus
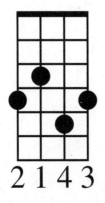
4fr.
1 1 4 2

Bdim7
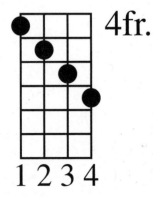
2 1 4 3

B+
4fr.
1 2 3 4

C CHORDS

C
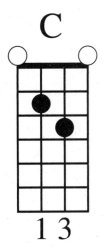
1 3

C
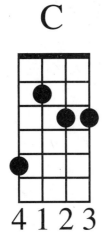
4 1 2 3

Cmaj7
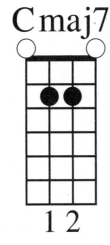
1 2

C6
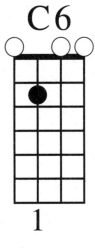
1

Cm
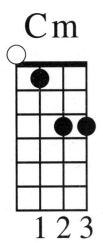
1 2 3

Cm
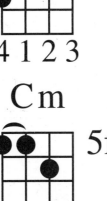
 5fr.
1 1 2 4

Cm7
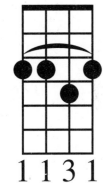
1 1 3 3

Cm6
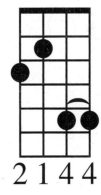
1 1 3 1

C7
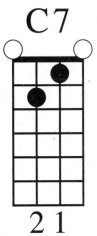
2 1

C7
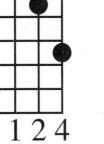
 5fr.
1 1 3 2

C9
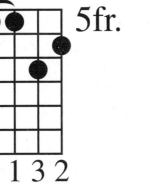
2 1 4 3

C13

2 1 4 4

Csus
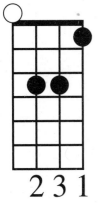
2 3 1

C7sus
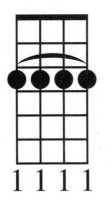
1 1 1 1

Cdim7
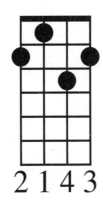
2 1 4 3

C+
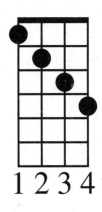
1 2 3 4

C♯ (D♭) CHORDS*

C♯
3fr.

4 1 2 3

C♯
6fr.

1 1 3 4

C♯maj7
3fr.

4 1 1 2

C♯6
6fr.

1 1 3 1

C♯m

4 1 2 3

C♯m
6fr.

1 1 2 4

C♯m7
6fr.

1 1 3 3

C♯m6
6fr.

1 1 3 1

C♯7

2 1 3 4

C♯7
6fr.

1 1 3 2

C♯9

2 1 4 3

C♯13

2 1 4 4

C♯sus

4 2 3 1

C♯7sus

1 1 1 1

C♯dim7

2 1 4 3

C♯+

1 2 3 4

*C♯ and D♭ are two names for the same note.

D CHORDS

D
2   3

D
1 3 4 1

Dmaj7
1 3 4 1

D6
1 3 1 1

Dm
2   1

Dm
2 3 4 1

Dm7
2 3 1

Dm6
2 3 1

D7
1 3 2

D7
1 3 2 1

D9
1 3 2

D13
4 3 1

Dsus
1   3

D7sus
1 2 3

Ddim7
1 3 2

D+
3fr.
1 2 3 4

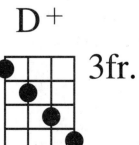

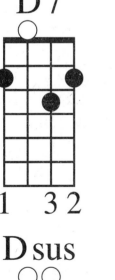
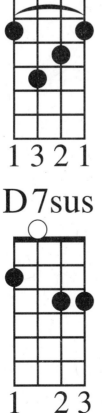

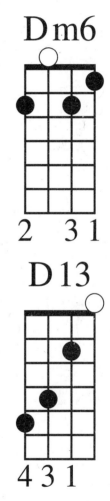
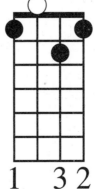
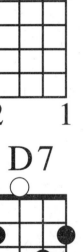
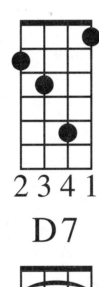

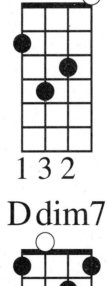
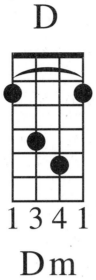

E♭ (D♯) CHORDS*

E♭
2 1 1 3

E♭
1 3 4 1

E♭maj7
2 1 3

E♭6
1 3 1 1

E♭m
3 1 1 2

E♭m
2 3 4 1

E♭m7
3 1 4 2

E♭m6
3 1 4 2

E♭7
2 1 4 3

E♭7
1 3 2 1

E♭9
2 4 3 1

E♭13
2 4 3 1

E♭sus
3 1 1 4

E♭7sus
1 4 2 3

E♭dim7
2 1 4 3

E♭+
1 2 3

*E♭ and D♯ are two names for the same note.

47

E CHORDS

E

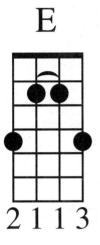

2 1 1 3

E

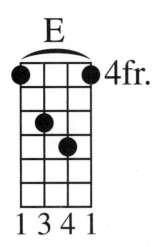

4fr.

1 3 4 1

Emaj7

3 1 2 4

E6

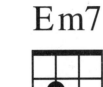

4fr.

1 3 1 1

Em

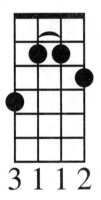

3 1 1 2

Em

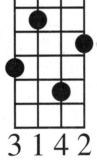

3fr.

2 3 4 1

Em7

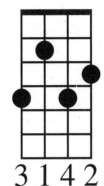

3 1 4 2

Em6

3 1 4 2

E7

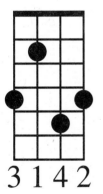

3 1 4 2

E7

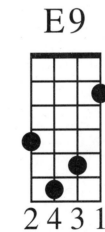

4fr.

1 3 2 4

E9

2 4 3 1

E13

2 4 3 1

Esus

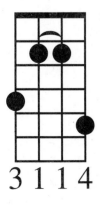

3 1 1 4

E7sus

2 1 3 4

Edim7

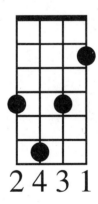

2 1 4 3

E+

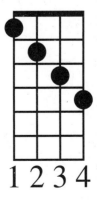

1 2 3 4

48

F CHORDS

F
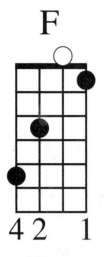
4 2   1

F

2 1 1 4

Fmaj7
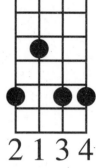
3 1

F6

2 1 3 4

Fm

3 1 1 2

Fm
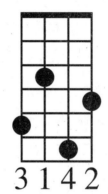 4fr.
2 3 4 1

Fm7

3 1 4 2

Fm6
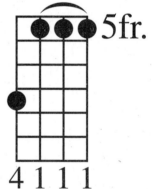
3 1 4 2

F7
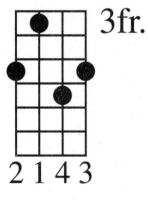 3fr.
2 1 4 3

F7
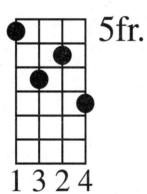 5fr.
1 3 2 4

F9
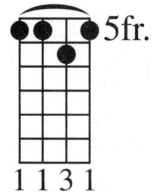 5fr.
1 1 3 1

F13
5fr.
4 1 1 1

Fsus
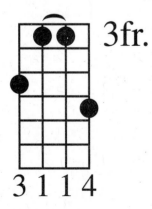 3fr.
3 1 1 4

F7sus
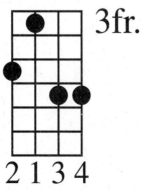 3fr.
2 1 3 4

Fdim7

2 1 4 3

F+
1 2 3 4

F♯ (G♭) CHORDS*

F♯

4 3 1 2

F♯
4fr.

2 1 1 3

F♯maj7

3 1 2 4

F♯6
4fr.

2 1 3 4

F♯m

4 2 1

F♯m
4fr.

3 1 1 2

F♯m7
4fr.

3 1 4 2

F♯m6
4fr.

3 1 4 2

F♯7
4fr.

2 1 4 3

F♯7
6fr.

1 3 2 1

F♯9
6fr.

1 1 3 1

F♯13
6fr.

4 1 1 1

F♯sus
4fr.

3 1 1 4

F♯7sus
4fr.

2 1 3 4

F♯dim7
4fr.

2 1 4 3

F♯+
3fr.

1 2 3 4

*F♯ and G♭ are two names for the same note.

G CHORDS

G
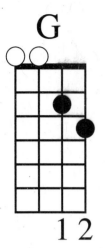
1 2

G
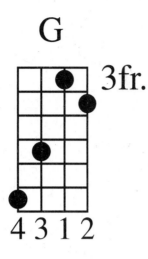
3fr.
4 3 1 2

Gmaj7
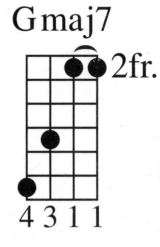
2fr.
4 3 1 1

G6
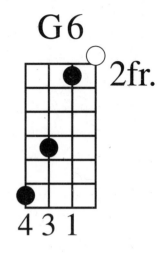
2fr.
4 3 1

Gm
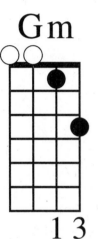
1 3

Gm

5fr.
3 1 1 2

Gm7
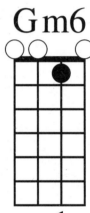
1 2

Gm6
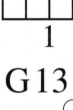
1

G7
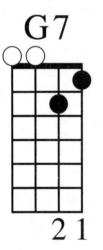
2 1

G7
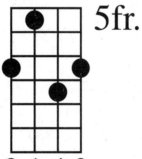
5fr.
2 1 4 3

G9
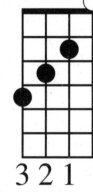
7fr.
1 1 3 1

G13

3 2 1

Gsus
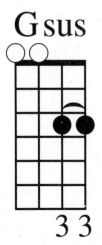
3 3

G7sus
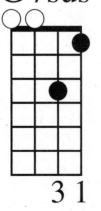
3 1

Gdim7

2 1 4 3

G⁺
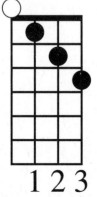
1 2 3

A♭ (G♯) CHORDS

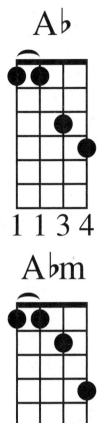
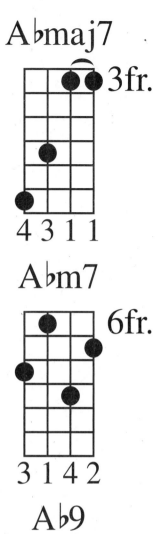
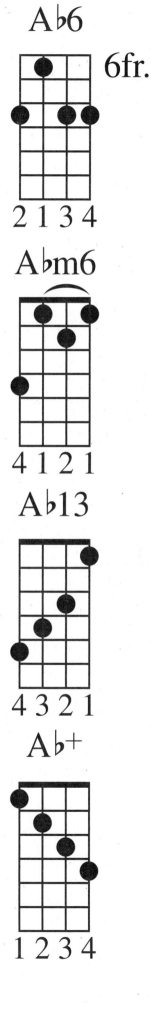
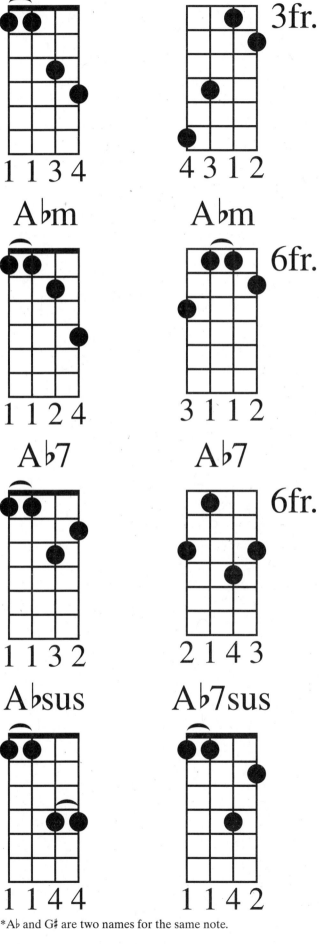

*A♭ and G♯ are two names for the same note.